It's Catching

Chicken Pox

Angela Royston

Heinemann Library
Chicago, Illinois

Designed by David Oakley/Arnos Design
Originated by Dot Gradations
Printed in Hong Kong, China

06 05 04 03 02
10 9 8 7 6 5 4 3 2 1

Library of Congress Cataloging-in-Publication Data
Royston, Angela.
     Chicken pox / Angela Royston.
         p. ; cm. -- (It's catching)
     Includes bibliographical references and index.
     ISBN 1-58810-226-2
     1. Chickenpox--Juvenile literature. [1. Chicken pox. 2. Diseases.]
     [DNLM: 1. Chickenpox--Juvenile Literature. WC 572 R892c 2001] I.
     Title. II. Series.

RC125 .R69 2001
616.9'14--dc21

                                     00-012832

Acknowledgments
The Publishers would like to thank the following for permission to reproduce photographs:
pp. 17, 26 Jennie Woodcock/Bubbles; p. 19 Gareth Boden; p. 24 John Callan/Shout; p. 5 Kevin Peterson/PhotoDisc; p. 29 Powerstock; p. 10 Sally and Richard Greenhill; Science Photo Library: pp. 4, 7 Dick Luria, 8 Eye of Science, 9, 14, 15, 16, 18 Mark Clarke, 12 Ken Cavanagh, 13, 22, 23, 25 P. Marazzi, 28; Stone: pp. 21 Klaus Lahnstein, 27 Lori Adamski Peek; Tony Stone: pp. 6 Jerome Tisne, 11 Bruce Ayres, 20 Dianne Fiumara.

Cover photograph reproduced with permission of Images.

Every effort has been made to contact copyright holders of any material reproduced in this book. Any omissions will be rectified in subsequent printings if notice is given to the Publisher.

Some words are shown in bold, **like this.** You can find out what they mean by looking in the glossary.

Contents

What Is Chicken Pox?

Chicken pox is an illness that gives you a **rash** of spots on your skin. This book is about chicken pox and how it affects you.

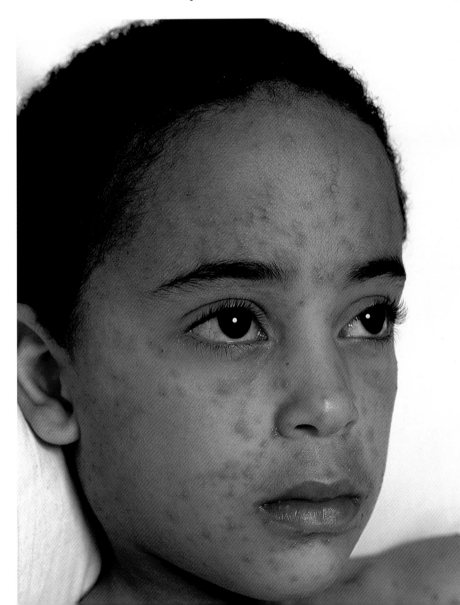

Some illnesses are **infectious.** This means that they are passed from one person to another. Chicken pox is infectious.

Healthy Skin

Skin protects your body in many different ways. It protects you from the harmful rays of the sun. Skin needs a lot of **sunscreen** to help keep it safe.

Skin also stops dirt and **germs** from getting inside your body. When you get hot, your skin sweats to help cool you down.

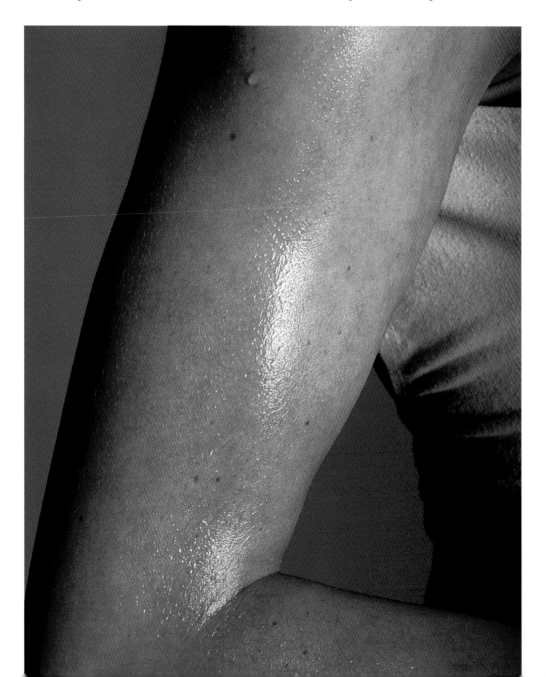

What Causes Chicken Pox?

Chicken pox is caused by a **virus.** When
the virus gets inside your body it can
make you ill. Viruses are so tiny that
you need a **microscope** to see them.

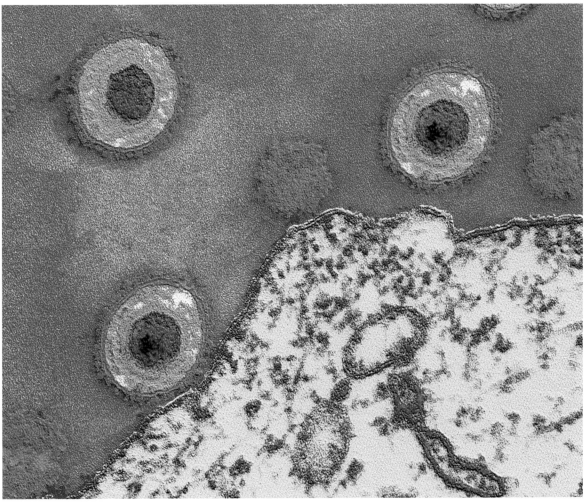

The chicken pox virus gives you spots on your skin, but not all spots are caused by chicken pox. A doctor can tell you if the spots you have are chicken pox.

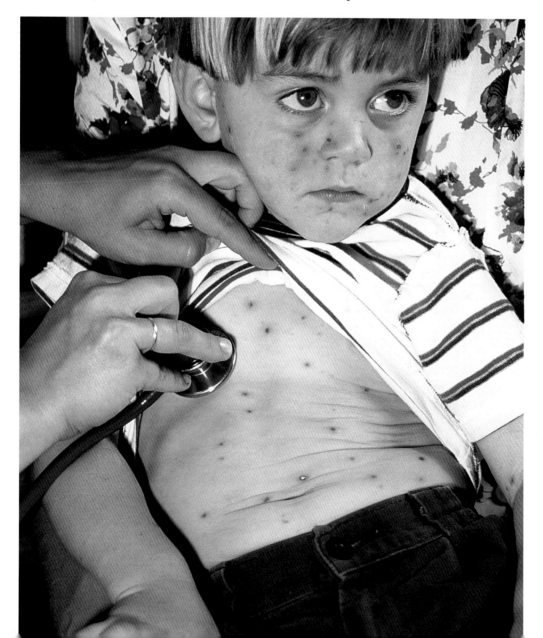

First Signs

It takes about ten days for the chicken pox **virus** to make you feel ill. Your bones may ache and you may have a **fever.**

This girl's father is using a **thermometer** to take her **temperature.** The thermometer will show whether her body is hotter than normal.

The Next Stage

You cannot tell if you have chicken pox until you get little red spots. They usually show up on the **chest** and back first. Later they may appear on your legs, arms, and face, too.

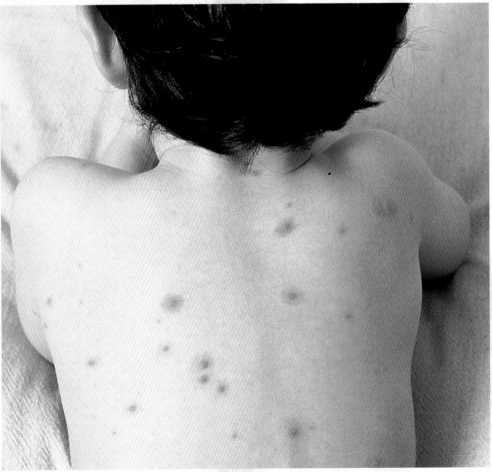

After several hours each spot changes to a small yellow **blister**. After a while, the blisters burst and dry up.

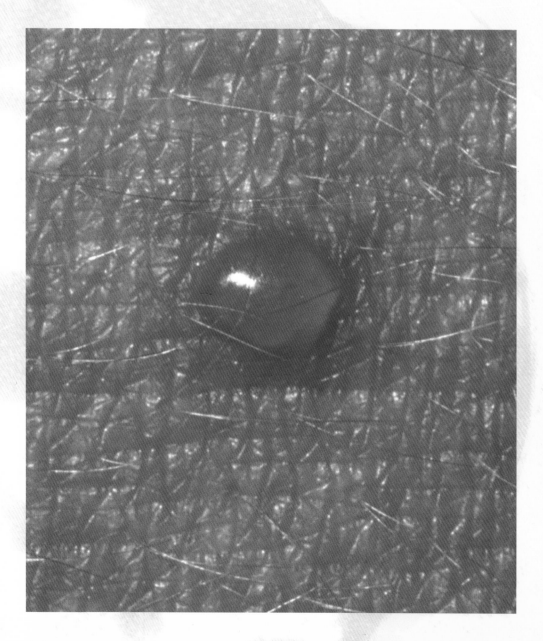

Don't Scratch!

Chicken pox **blisters** can be very itchy, but it is important not to scratch them. If you do scratch, they may become **infected** by other **germs.**

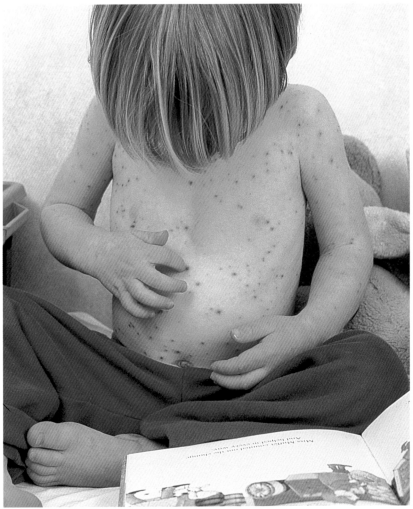

If that happens, the doctor will give you a cream to kill the germs causing the infection. If you are very unlucky, infected blisters can leave a **scar** on your skin.

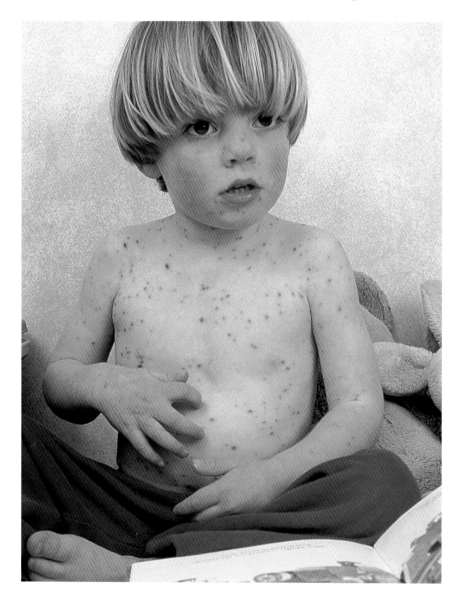

How Chicken Pox Is Spread

If you have chicken pox, you breathe out millions of chicken pox **germs** with every breath. So, someone else may breathe the **virus** in.

People can also catch the virus if they touch the liquid from the **blisters.** You are **infectious** until the last blister has crusted over and formed a **scab.**

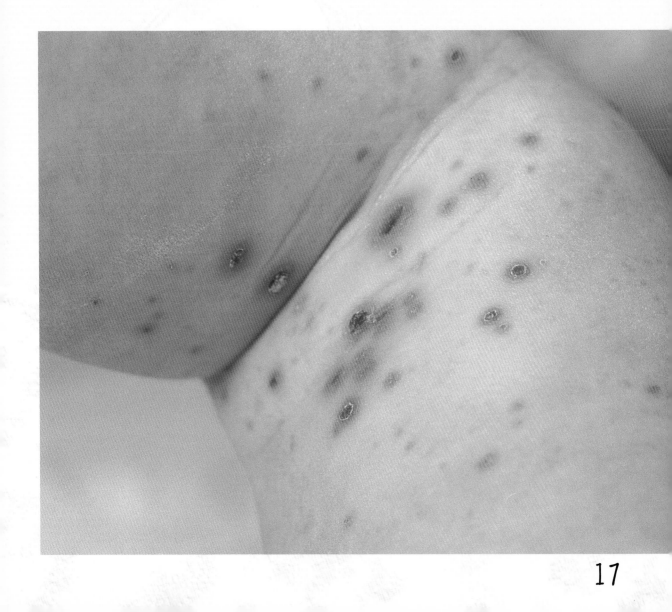

Treatment

There is no **medicine** that will make chicken pox get better faster. Your body gets better on its own, but it takes one or two weeks.

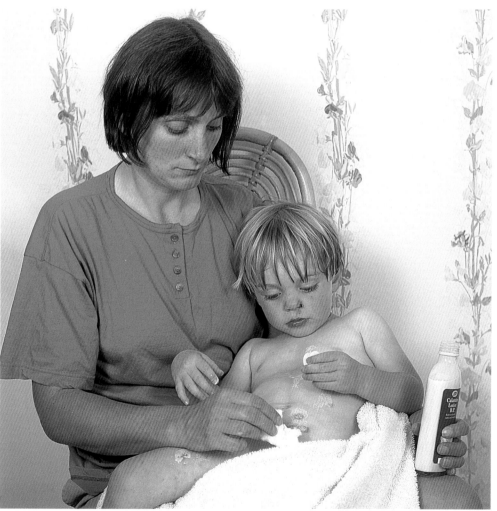

You can use **calamine** lotion to make the **blisters** less itchy. A large spoonful of **baking soda** mixed into a warm bath also helps.

Chicken Pox Can Be Dangerous

Chicken pox is not a serious disease if you catch it when you are a child, but it can be a serious illness in very young babies.

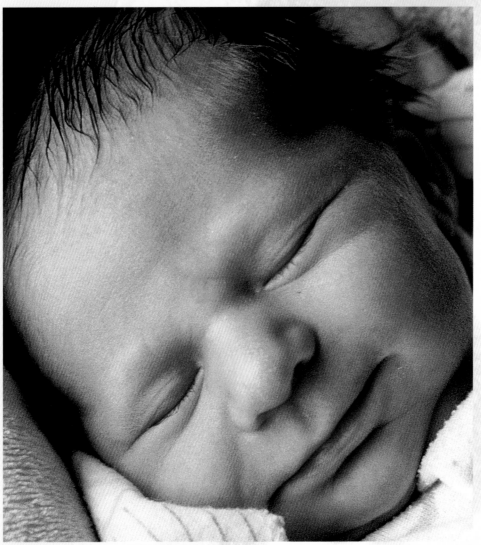

People who are very old or already very sick may also suffer badly from chicken pox. Their bodies may not be strong enough to fight the disease.

Avoiding Chicken Pox

If you do not want to get chicken pox, you should stay away from people who have it. Babies and very old people can be **injected** to keep them from getting the illness.

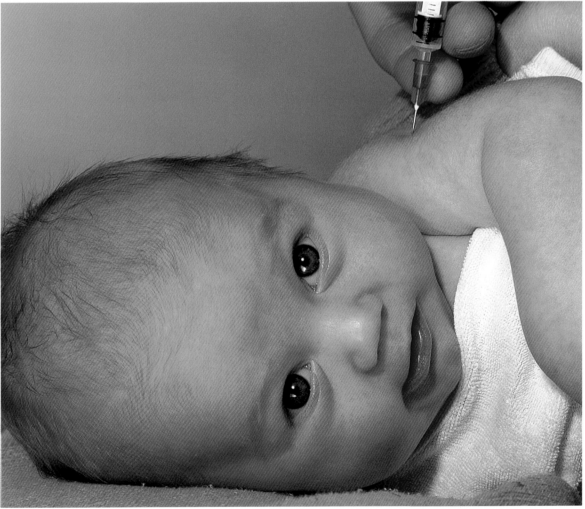

Once you have had chicken pox, you will not catch it again. Your body will have made special **blood cells** like this one. They kill the chicken pox **virus** before it makes you ill.

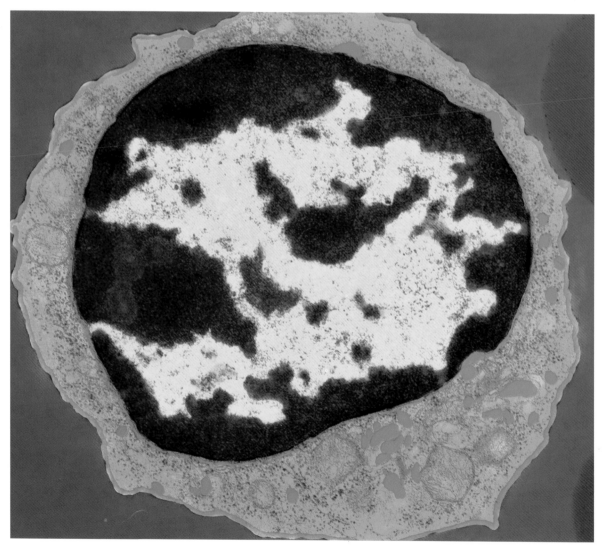

Immunity

Children who catch chicken pox are affected much less than tiny babies and adults. Many parents want their children to catch chicken pox so that they become **immune** when they are young. So, they let them play with friends who have it.

With a few people, the **virus** stays in the body and causes another itchy **rash** many years later. This rash is called **shingles.**

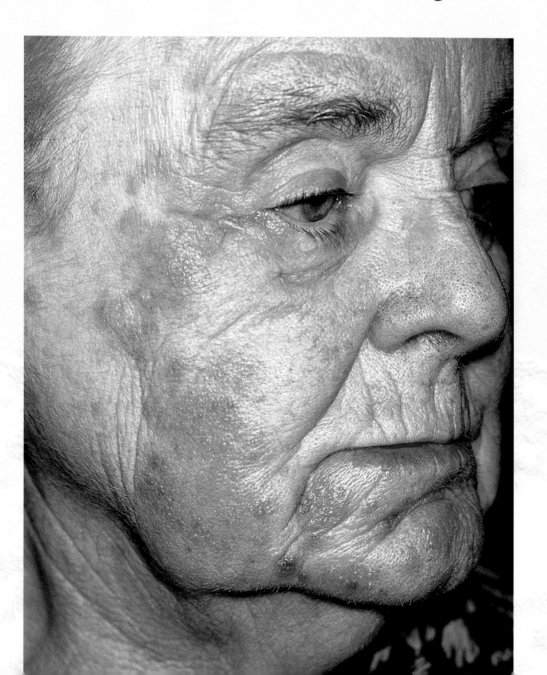

Staying Healthy

The best way to avoid many illnesses is to live a healthy life. Eat healthy food and get plenty of fresh air.

Keep yourself clean and wash your hands often.
Get lots of exercise and plenty of sleep.

Think About It!

Ben has noticed that he has a **rash** on his skin. How can he tell if it is chicken pox?*

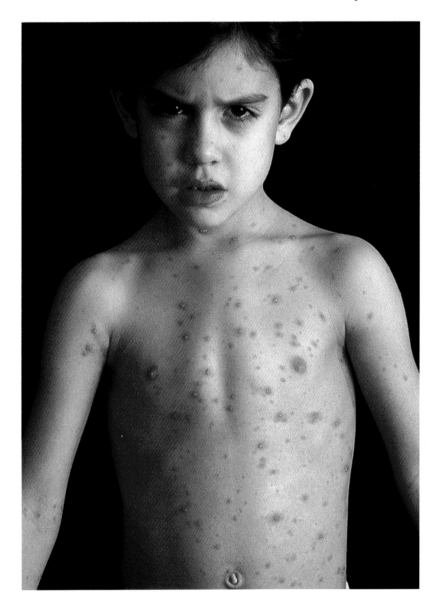

John says that you catch chicken pox
when you touch someone's chicken pox
blisters. David says you have to breathe
in the **germs.** Who is right?*

*Read page 30 to find out.

Answers

Page 28

If the **rash** is made up of red spots that turn to yellow **blisters,** Ben probably has chicken pox. He must show them to a doctor, who will be able to tell him if he has chicken pox.

Page 29

Both John and David are right.

Stay Healthy and Safe!

1. Always tell an adult if you feel sick or think there is something wrong with you.

2. Never take any **medicine** or use any **ointment** unless it is given to you by an adult you trust.

3. Remember, the best way to stay healthy and safe is to eat good food, drink lots of water, keep clean, exercise, and get lots of sleep.

Glossary

baking soda   a white powder used in cooking and medicine

blister   small bubble of liquid under the skin

blood cell   tiny building block that forms your blood; your blood has millions of blood cells

calamine   used to relieve the itching and pain of the skin

chest   part of the front of the body between the neck and the stomach

fever   when the temperature of your blood becomes hotter than usual

germ   tiny living thing that can make you ill if it gets inside your body

immune   protection from catching an infection

infected   suffering from an illness caused by germs

infectious   can be passed from one person to another and can make you sick

injected   to have something pushed into the body by a syringe, often to help prevent illness

medicine   something used to treat or prevent an illness

microscope   something that makes very small things look big enough to see

ointment   oily cream that often contains medicine and is rubbed onto the skin

rash   a breaking out of the skin with red spots

scab   hard covering made when the liquid inside a chicken pox blister spills out and dries

scar   mark left on the skin by a deep cut or an infected chicken pox spot

shingles   illness that can be caused many years later by chicken pox viruses staying in the body long after the illness has gone

sunscreen   substance used on the skin to help protect it from the sun's harmful radiation

temperature   measure of how hot or cold something is

thermometer   something that measures temperature

virus   tiny living thing that can make you sick if it gets inside your body

Index

More Books to Read

Hundley, David H. *Viruses.* Vero Beach, Fla.: Rourke Press, 1998.

Weitzman, Elizabeth. *Let's Talk about Having Chicken Pox.* New York: Rosen Publishing Group, 1997.

Wixom, Tedi T. *Trevor's Red Spots: Chicken Pox Time.* Salt Lake City, Utah: T N T Books, 1996.